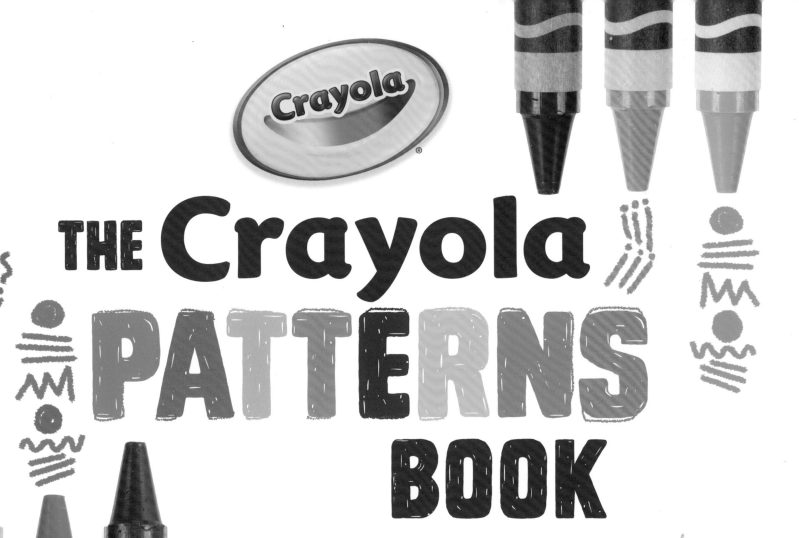

THE Crayola PATTERNS BOOK

MARI SCHUH

LERNER PUBLICATIONS ◆ MINNEAPOLIS

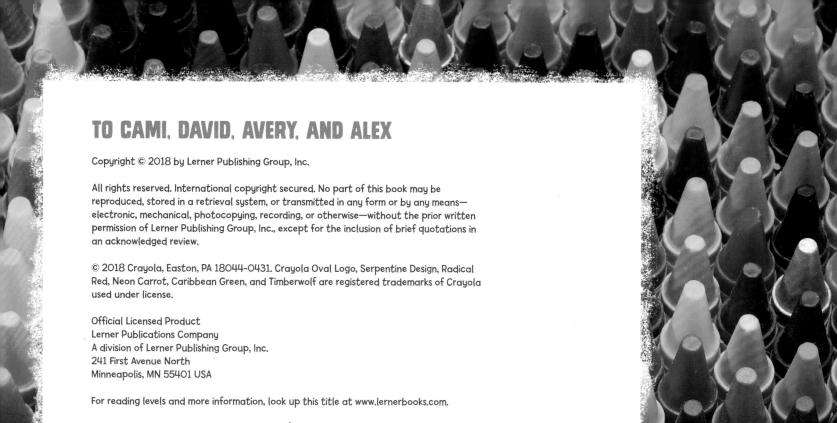

TO CAMI, DAVID, AVERY, AND ALEX

Official Licensed Product
Lerner Publications Company
A division of Lerner Publishing Group, Inc.
241 First Avenue North
Minneapolis, MN 55401 USA

For reading levels and more information, look up this title at www.lernerbooks.com.

Main body text set in Billy Infant Regular 24/30.
Typeface provided by SparkyType.

Library of Congress Cataloging-in-Publication Data

Names: Schuh, Mari C., 1975- author.
Title: The Crayola patterns book / by Mari Schuh.
Description: Minneapolis : Lerner Publications, 2017. | Series: Crayola concepts | Includes
    bibliographical references and index. | Audience: Ages 4-9. | Audience: K to grade 3.
Identifiers: LCCN 2016049248 (print) | LCCN 2016050341 (ebook) | ISBN 9781512432855
    (lb : alk. paper) | ISBN 9781512455700 (pb : alk. paper) | ISBN 9781512449266 (eb pdf)
Subjects: LCSH: Pattern perception—Juvenile literature. | Crayons—Juvenile literature.
Classification: LCC BF294 .S37 2017 (print) | LCC BF294 (ebook) | DDC 701/.8—dc23

LC record available at https://lccn.loc.gov/2016049248

Manufactured in the United States of America
1-41816-23776-2/1/2017

Table of Contents

Patterns All Around   4

People and Patterns   6

Patterns in Nature   14

So Many Patterns   20

World of Colors   22

Glossary   23

To Learn More   24

Index   24

PATTERNS ALL AROUND

Our world is full of patterns. Patterns are colors, lines, and shapes that repeat.

PEOPLE AND PATTERNS

Some patterns repeat shapes.

Many circles make a polka-dot pattern.

Create your own pattern by repeating shapes. What colors will you use?

Some patterns repeat colors. Bright colors make exciting patterns in so many ways!

Red, yellow, blue. Red, yellow, blue.
Can you find patterns way up high?

Some patterns repeat lines.

Zigzag lines make a big, bold pattern.

What other kinds of lines can you draw
to make a pattern?

Cloth is made by weaving threads together.

The threads cross over and under one another.
They form a pattern.

Use your favorite colors to draw a pattern of stripes. How does it look?

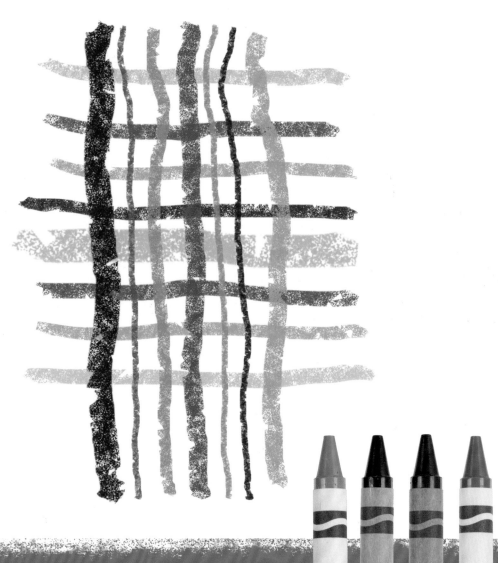

PATTERNS IN NATURE

Some animals wear a pattern!

Zebras are covered in black-and-white stripes.

Some stripes are wide. Other stripes are thin.

Patterns in nature go around and around!

Spiral patterns are curvy.

Create your own spiral patterns with crayons or markers. Can you draw many spirals in one?

Some patterns fall from the sky!

Snowflakes have symmetry. Each half of the snowflake has the same pattern.

SO MANY PATTERNS

Patterns are everywhere!

Where can you find patterns?

WORLD OF COLORS

Patterns come in all kinds of colors. Here are some of the Crayola® crayon colors in this book. Can you find them in the photos?

GOLDENROD

CADET BLUE

RADICAL RED

NEON CARROT

MAGENTA

CARIBBEAN GREEN

GREEN YELLOW

TIMBERWOLF

GLOSSARY

bold: standing out in a noticeable way

pattern: colors, lines, or shapes that repeat in a certain order

repeat: to appear or happen over and over again

spiral: a pattern that winds around a center point in a circle

stripe: a line or long section of color

symmetry: having two sides, or halves, that look the same

thread: a strand of material that is used for sewing

weaving: making cloth, baskets, or other objects by passing threads or fabric strips over and under one another

zigzag: a line that has short, sharp turns

TO LEARN MORE

BOOKS

Bluemel Oldfield, Dawn. *Patterns at the Seashore.* New York: Bearport, 2015. Read about all the kinds of patterns found on the seashore.

Brocket, Jane. *Spotty, Stripy, Swirly: What Are Patterns?* Minneapolis: Millbrook Press, 2012. Read this book to find all sorts of patterns, from food and buildings to clothes and nature.

Felix, Rebecca. *Patterns in the City.* Ann Arbor, MI: Cherry Lake, 2015. Learn about the many patterns that can be found in the big city.

WEBSITES

Pattern Game
http://www.abcya.com/fuzz_bugs_patterns.htm
Play a fun game completing patterns of colors at this website.

Piece-Together Patterns
http://www.crayola.com/crafts/piecetogether-patterns-craft/
Color and cut out shapes, and then use them to design your own patterns!

INDEX

cloth, 12
color, 4, 7–8, 13

line, 4, 10–11

shapes, 4, 6–7
spiral, 16–17
stripes, 13, 14–15
symmetry, 19

PHOTO ACKNOWLEDGMENTS

The images in this book are used with the permission of: © iStockphoto.com/jallfree, p. 5 (top left); © iStockphoto.com/Nickos, p. 5 (top right); © iStockphoto.com/Spiderplay, p. 5 (bottom left); © Sparkia/Dreamstime.com, p. 5 (bottom right); © iStockphoto.com/WestLight, p. 5 (center); © iStockphoto.com/Sevulya p. 6; © Andy Piatt/Dreamstime.com, pp. 8–9; © Vesilvio/Dreamstime.com, p. 10; Africa Studio/Shutterstock.com, p. 12; IVASHstudio/Shutterstock.com, p. 15; © Henrik Sorensen/Getty Images, p. 17; © Udra11/Dreamstime.com, p. 19; © iStockphoto.com/ Judith Dzierzawa, p. 20; Letterberry/Shutterstock.com, p. 21 (top left); © iStockphoto.com/fstop123, p. 21 (top right); © iStockphoto.com/Panama7, p. 21 (bottom left); liza1979/Shutterstock.com, p. 21 (bottom right); © iStockphoto.com/IgorKirillov, p. 21 (center).

Cover: © iStockphoto.com/GlobalP (dogs); © iStockphoto.com/JacobH (tulips); © Letterberry/Shutterstock.com (tomatoes).

LERNER
SOURCE

Expand learning beyond the printed book. Download free, complementary educational resources for this book from our website, www.lernerresource.com.